GHOST HANDS

N. S. Thompson

The Melos Press

First published in 2020
by The Melos Press
38 Palewell Park
London SW14 8JG

melospress.blogspot.com

ACKNOWLEDGMENTS are due to the following publications where many of
these poems first appeared: *Able Muse* (USA), *Birmingham Poetry Review*
(USA), *New Walk, Oxford Poetry, Sewanee Theological Review* (USA), *The
Spectator*. 'The Women in Delft' first appeared in the pamphlet *Mr Larkin
on Photography* (Red Squirrel, 2016).
My thanks to the editors concerned.

Printed by The Melos Press

CONTENTS

Hunters in the Snow   5
A Dutch Master   6
The Women in Delft   7
Oxford as Modern Art   9
19th Century Nudes   10
Ghost Hands   12
Ruskin in Ambleside   14
For Art's Sake   15

HUNTERS IN THE SNOW
after Bruegel

This is the world we know and do not know,
　　　The village as it always is,
But what about those mountains over there?

They seem to point to finitude, the end of things,
　　　But we are in the foreground and preoccupied
With trudging infinitely through the snow.

A DUTCH MASTER

A windmill turns as cattle stoop to drink:
A revolution in the world of art.
Behind them, slanting grey and silver trace
A steeple pointing to a passing cloud
That covers up the distant troubling space
God leaves; instead, I add a touch of gloss
To hocks and dripping muzzles as they sink
Beneath the brooding ripples, leaving out
The gadding flies that halo round the bowed
Heads, taking it as pardonable the loss
That only makes the landscape more devout
And gives reality another start.

THE WOMEN IN DELFT
Johannes Van Der Meer

We look at them expectantly: a room
With balance held, a string of pearls, a hand
Placed on the virginal, or there a letter
Clutched to the breast; these women keep
The gentle art of looking artfully
Revealed, yet hidden in the art of space.

They seem absorbed in it and yet leave space
For eyes to linger on them in that room
And wonder what the painter artfully
Kept in or out, things under hand
Or *underhand*? The surfaces still keep
Us guessing. What could be in that one's letter

Or that one's balance? And why does he let her
Appear to weigh up in that pregnant space
Such a wealth of meaning only to keep
It from us in that sunlit room?
Are we – the viewers – meant to have a hand
In them and come to see what artfully

Has been concealed? That *View of Delft* is artfully
Conceived yet *not* depicted to the letter
But *deftly* rearranged, the painter's hand
Adding the unknown of space,
A brooding sky providing all the room
To rise above the secrets buildings keep…

Or take elsewhere that crenellated keep
Of brick (its outside walls so artfully

Salt-leached) allowing us again the room
To wonder if they hold that letter
Or else the string of pearls in all that space
Held in *The Little Street*. Whose was the hand

That let the children out of doors or hand
That pressed the collars, urging them to keep
The clothes clean, as she hurriedly made space
To meet the lover artfully
Returned from sea or merchant whose last letter
Had news that left her trembling in that room?

How artfully he let us have a hand
In them and keep us guessing in the space
Between a letter and a sunlit room.

OXFORD AS MODERN ART

A college collage by De Chirico,
The High looks populated by Magritte
(Raindrops of people); coloured by Rousseau,
 Botanic Gardens dreaming green complete

The picture; framed by walls of Cotswold stone,
Tourists walk outlined in light by stark
Shades, quilted jackets and Expressionist tone
Where Giacometti figures grace a park.

19th CENTURY NUDES

Such flawless women! How they make you sigh:
      Hairless, but with the heads held high,
      The heads, at least, abundantly in curls
And tresses, but the bodies white as pearls

Show nothing else. Of course, the Greeks did much
      The same, no wisp or trace to touch
      Or linger on, or put a finger on,
No gaudy colour left where sunlight shone.

Now only dusty galleries that hold
      Them colourless and chaste, the fold
      Of arm or leg preserving from the sight
What anyway would show as ghostly, white.

And so the painters imitated art
      And, classically trained, would not depart
      From what they saw almost divine,
A bloodless beauty, chaste and crystalline.

And if that girl with pitcher full of water
      Looks innocent, she was a cheap trull's daughter
      With all her edges smoothed and clefts withdrawn,
Simply aesthetic, barely human, shorn

Of Mother Nature's covering. Ruskin
      Apparently was shocked to find the skin
      Had mats of hair over the private parts.
A legend? Well, if history departs

From fact, that's nothing new and Winckelmann
        Was equally beguiled by the wan
        Complexions: if Greeks liked the body bare,
Then art showed them with not a trace of hair

Apart from what would tumble from the shoulders.
        The rest was smoothly polished and as cold as
        Ice. A strange way for fine art to behave
And begs the question: did the ancients shave?

GHOST HANDS

Sant'Apollinare Nuovo, Ravenna

Your hands brush marble, feel impelled
    To touch where crisp cold tesserae
        Compose a fine array
Of arches that once held
    A gallery of courtiers with gifts they gave
A throne in mosaic palace down a long cool nave.
    Now strung between the arches like a tapestry
    Hang folds that robbed Theoderic of his majesty.

Yes, it was curtains for him and his court,
    Walls cleansed of every sign
That Arian's heresy was taught
    Here. Now the floating drapery seems to swell
        Like jaunty washing on a line
Where once the string of courtiers spanned arcades,
    Except where three white columns tell
        The legacy that history deceives
Below the capstones of acanthus leaves
That crown the columns where the accolades
    Were laid. His palace, set above, still stands
        Mosaic, but the shape his person made
        A formless mass, betrayed
By history, but for those three trunkless hands
    Once joyful, welcoming, now sadly raised
        In permanent farewell to what the Trinity erased.

NOTE

Decorative mosaics of Theoderic the Great (454-526AD) and his Arian court were removed as heretical from Sant'Apollinare by order of Justinian. The work left three hands on columns in the palace arcade belonging, it is thought, to members of a court procession.

RUSKIN IN AMBLESIDE

Stock Ghyll Force

Iron railings. Iron railways.
 Hopes bitterly withdrawn.
  A parasol is twirled.
 A lady is beguiled

By foaming white cascades. While in a daze,
 He leans and thinks... Had Leonardo drawn
  Such pools? What secrets in the world!
 "Yes, look, dear. Nature; it is wild."

FOR ART'S SAKE...
An Essay in Verse

I

This essay is for everyone, the door
      Is open for you, drawing out a line
To hook the general reader in, well, more
      Or less. The visual arts were once termed 'fine';
That is, 'refined' until all art went poor
      And gold and jewels could no longer shine
On walls, except in works by Gustav Klimt
(For whom no ornament was ever skimped)

And like all essays it may take some time
      To settle down until it hits the note
It wants, but then it is composed in rhyme,
      Part satire, part attempt at antidote
Against today's artistic paradigm
      That loves to wear a motley-coloured coat
To work, but surely hits a paradox
When seeking publics that it merely shocks.

And this goes back historically to when
      The world was dealing with a bourgeoisie
Created by the rise of businessmen,
      A class that artists quickly came to see
In two ways; firstly, as the specimen
      Of what was deemed 'respectability',
That blank façade that hides a multitude
Of sins (some of which can be very rude);

And, secondly, as a target fair to mock
      For its *nouveau* pretensions off the Bourse
And on it; but while artists loved to cock
      A snook at them from attic rooms, the *force*

Majeur that kept their easels out of hock
      Was the business model they could endorse
With Art declared a new commodity,
No matter if it seemed an oddity.

Did this initiate the interest in
      Creating works of art from simple trash?
Machines had taken print out for a spin
      But Futurism soon produced a Trash
Can School of pure reality, the sin
      Was selling that reality for cash,
But artists found an awful lot of trade
In marketing the art of readymade.

Today we see the same relationship
      As plutocrats, celebs and marketeers
Compete for work come from a rubbish tip,
      Material not meant to last for years,
And yet's the thing that makes the markets flip
      And auctions thrive. Has no one any fears
About an artwork that may never last?
It's readymade… that's ready to sell fast.

We see the art of light bulbs, plastic used
      Around a dangling fluorescent strip,
Which makes curators who are very shrewd
      Think twice before they take on stewardship
Of works that might become unscrewed, unglued
      Or at the mercy of the microchip:
A new twist on curators and the light
Bulb joke. Let's hope they learn to get it right.

II

What's tempting for an artist starting out
      Is swallowing the host of fairy tales
That hagiography still loves to spout;
      Unfortunately, this will add to sales
And helps a critic's prose have added clout
      When measuring out a life in coffin nails,
Maintaining artists have to burn like flame.
But flames go out as quickly as they came.

Art is theatrical and uses sleight
      Of hand, reminding us it is illusion
That paradoxically will underwrite
      Artists' methods to illustrate profusion
And life's abundance as they trick the sight,
      But from an audience you need collusion
And understanding art's a serious game
Without which play it can seem very tame…

Who was it said that to survive the first
      (Say) forty years becomes the hardest part
For any artist? Yes, you'll find you're cursed
      If you seek cash and credit out of art,
Far better it should flow out unrehearsed
      And seem to come straight from the heart.
But this too is a fiction. You should know
That spontaneity is only show.

So, am I rooting for longevity?
      You bet. Consider working for the long
Haul, not sell short your creativity:
      Youth – metaphorically – can use the tongue

To pull a face at sensitivity,
Using an organ makes the gesture strong,
But if sensationalism's only shock,
How long will it survive in history's dock?

Hokusai, Rembrandt, Hockney, William Blake
Created masterpieces at an age
That fashion today would have us forsake,
A sober thought that should bring on a rage
To shame the fashion makers. May they ache
With sorrow as they come to see as sage
The thought from Darwin that the last is best,
If evolution can be used as test.

There is another side to this, no doubt,
That those the Muses favour must die young:
They writhe in inspiration, twist and shout
With prophecies and if they die unsung
Then trust a band of followers devout
To say the telephone of art has rung
For them and is immutable, the sound
Is youth and fury and it seems profound...

But why demand of youth that it must rush
On blindly as if desperate to be done?
Youth has to find itself among the crush
Of hopefuls and pretenders to the throne
Of art and it takes years to master brush,
Paint, ink or felt tip pen. Is there a gun
Placed at your temples threatening you to start?
The avant-garde, *bien sûr*, thinks *this* is art:

Walk blindfold for one week and so instruct
        Beholders what life's like without your eyes
To see; or every evening reconstruct
        A masterpiece but in some other guise
As sprayed graffiti or in wire, conduct
        A symphony by throwing custard pies...
The avant-garde must lead the way and walk
The walk alone. But what is it bar talk?

Or why not have a MOMA Open Night?
        Free bicycles that everyone can ride
On special gangways leading to each sight,
        While overhead the strip lights are denied:
The public moves by means of cycle light
        And to CCTV will be decried
A stream of cyclists carrying art's spark
Like deep-sea anglerfishes in the dark.

This view without explanatory text
        Saves energy, its attitude correct
Environmentally, but leaves perplexed
        Minds that experientially connect
Together in not knowing what comes next
        And powerless, too, to know what to expect.
You only have a beam of light and bell
And circle in a parody of hell.

One myth is true, that artists tend to suffer,
        Yes, both the profligate and self-enclosed,
I wonder if it really makes you tougher
        To face the opposition you're exposed
To... well, the trick is to enjoy – enough – a
        Considerable span of years, then be proposed

For membership of top academies,
And finally create just what you please.

Well, so much for the artist suffering pain:
        Van Gogh comes tops perhaps for being cursed
Here, classed by some as practically insane.
        I would not say he was the very worst
Among the artists of a similar strain,
        It would be fun to think who was the first…
Prize for inflicting wounds, there is Gaugin –
But if we go back where it all began,

We find a murderer! Caravaggio
        Was highly skilled depicting pain and sweat,
A skill that called for some *coraggio*
        In dishing out the violence when he met
A rival, but the *bell'oltraggio*
        Brought him Christ's passion after Olivet,
Sparing none of the mountain of offence.
But Crucifixions spared no one expense.

For centuries the sufferings of the Son
        Of Man showing nothing but a stream of gore
That left no doubt what six-inch nails had done,
        While winged angels rising by the score
Wore costumes in which threads of gold were spun,
        But riches were supposed to foster awe,
At least upon the altarpiece of Ghent
We see the patron's money was well spent.

Van Eyck preferred a sacrificial lamb
      To pour its blood into a golden cup,
A metaphoric way to say "I am
      The Resurrection and the Life" and up
The soulful feelings go, the diaphragm
      Expands and your whole being wants to sup
Of Paradise like Coleridge's seer
Then on for *pommes frites* and a Belgian beer.

Perhaps today our palates are too full,
      Velasquez's 'Old Woman Poaching Eggs'
Appears too soft and humble for the pull
      And wrench of pathos; sniffing up the dregs
Of low life makes the everyday quite dull,
      Where it should make us thankful for the legs
That carry us and, yes, our daily bread
Without which we are very surely dead.

But I would say that pathos is alive –
      Do we not empathise and love and feel
Emotional responses, jump or dive
      With pleasure or despair? Why should we seal
Ourselves up, always cool? Let feelings thrive
      And let us put the passion back, surreal
Or real, or hyperreal… and then there's wit
With which to temper it; well, just a bit.

III

It never ceases to amaze me how
      Contemporary art goes hand in glove
With marketing and sales and yet somehow
      They say 'experimental' art's above
All lucrative concerns. And so we bow
      Down, thinking artists do it for the love
Of pushing boundaries, creating poise
Between philosophy and lots of noise.

Of course, there's pressure in the market place
      And feeling you must keep up to produce
The goods, but then we wonder "Where's the race?"
      "What is it?" and, above all, "what's its use?"
Experiment is fine, but why debase
      One's talent? After all, there's no excuse
In saying people like the mediocre,
It's like a card sharp cheating folk at poker.

Should art be elevated? Don't we love
      To be seduced by it and educated
All in one go? It need not be a grove
      In some Arcadia, stuck up and inflated,
Or palace or a turbine house all mauve.
      Can High Reality be reinstated
Along with painters *painting* humble states,
Not piles of underwear or plastic plates?

But then I love a collage by Kurt Schwitters,
      Max Ernst, Georges Braque and all the 20s men
(Apologies, there were no female sitters
      To grace this portrait group, at least not then,

O'Keefe apart). But what gives me the jitters
        Regarding this creative regimen
(Reacting to prevailing nihilism
By dosing it with humour through art's prism)

Is seeing those subversive gestures melt
        Away to specious imitations made
Of wax and fat and even roofing felt.
        What are they anymore but a tirade
Against the kind of art that we once knelt
        Or stood transfixed before? But this crusade
Has long enjoyed its victory: have we gone
To sleep? Surely it's time that art moved on?

And surely art can be inspired again
        And draw (or paint) us back to mystery – in
The sense of marvelling that brush or pen
        Or graphite point can lead to genuine
Appreciation of how (now and then)
        We see not darkly but through hyaline
The gravity of all the universe
Appearing manifold, splendid, diverse?

We hear that after Rothko art was changed
        Irrevocably; with the holocaust
Art could not cope with something so deranged
        It beggared all description. So we forced
Ourselves to look at blocks of colour ranged
        With pigment looking like a car's exhaust.
The drizzles of a Jackson Pollock raised
A smile, but Rothko's art is what they praised.

When art's down to performing constant tricks
        Without coordinating hand and eye,

Assuming that an audience gets its kicks
  From hints and winks and innuendos on the sly
And what is nothing but a 'pile of bricks'
  Or 'unmade bed' or 'two fried eggs' I try
To see its purely formal terms of shape…
The daily press sees nothing more than jape.

Today it seems the tail end wags the dog
  And not a Staffordshire in porcelain.
We see not clearly but in a fog,
  Repeating old experiments again
And then again. It could be there's a cog
  That needs replacing. Artists, critics, when
Will you return to what is artistry
Instead of nothing more than sophistry?

So here it is, an essay that's addressed
  To you, art lovers, also anyone
Who cares to read *ottava rima* pressed
  In service to a little sense of fun
To save art from its permanent arrest
  In false pretensions and the overdone
Experiment. Forget about what's "Cool"
And get back in the swim, inside the pool

Of knowledge and ability unique
  To those who demonstrate the craft of art
– Or, better put, the art of craft – and seek
  To privilege the human spirit for a start
And not as irremediably weak.
  So here's to art as something rather smart
And definitely worth its *matières,*
The trouble that it takes to make us care.